Days, Weeks, and Months

Written by Ann H. Matzke

Rourke Educational Media
rourkeeducationalmedia.com

Scan for Related Titles and Teacher Resources

www.rourkeeducationalmedia.com

PHOTO CREDITS: Cover © Lisa Thornberg; Title Page © Marcogovel, pupunkkop; Page 3 © yalcinsonat1; Page 4 © RuthBlack; Page 5 © Hughstoneian; Page 6 © Rastan; Page 7 © Logovski; Page 8 © CEFutcher; Page 9 © maska82; Page 16 © kate_sept2004; Page © 17 ISerg ; Page 18 © ogergo, Page 19 © Lemony, Kanate; Page 20 © pamspix ; Page 21 © Brainsil; Page 22 © Mark Evans; Page 23 © Michaeljung

Edited by Jill Sherman

Cover design by Tara Raymo

Interior design by Jen Thomas

Library of Congress PCN Data

Days, Weeks, and Months / Ann H. Matzke
(Little World Math)
ISBN 978-1-62169-887-6 (hard cover)
ISBN 978-1-62169-782-4 (soft cover)
ISBN 978-1-62169-986-6 (e-Book)
Library of Congress Control Number: 2013936804

Rourke Educational Media
Printed in the United States of America,
North Mankato, Minnesota

Rourke Educational Media

rourkeeducationalmedia.com

customerservice@rourkeeducationalmedia.com • PO Box 643328 Vero Beach, Florida 32964

How many days until the birthday party?
Shh! It's a surprise.

The birthday party is on April 11.

It's hard to wait even one day.

A day is 24 hours.

That is the time it takes Earth to spin around once on its axis.

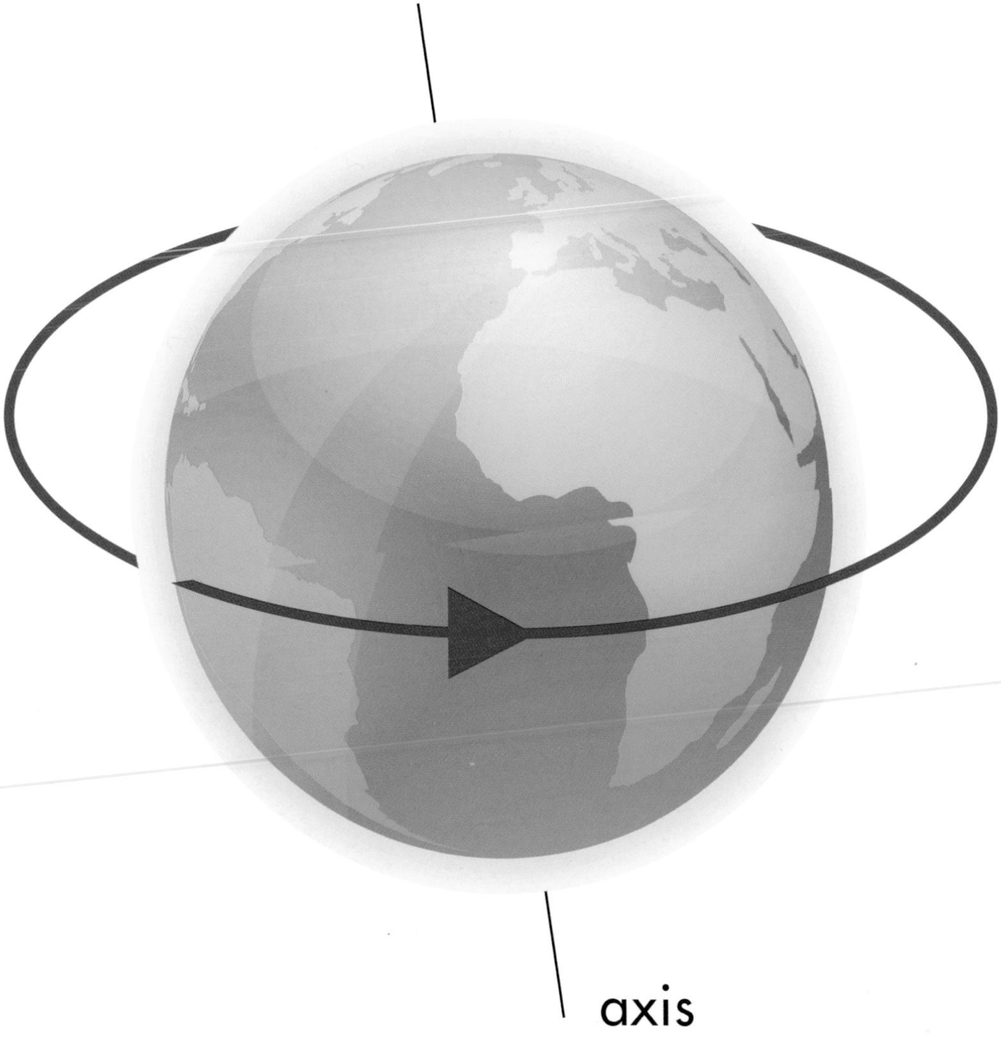

During the day, we work and play.

At night, it's time to sleep.

Together, 7 days makes a week.

Sunday is the first day of the week.

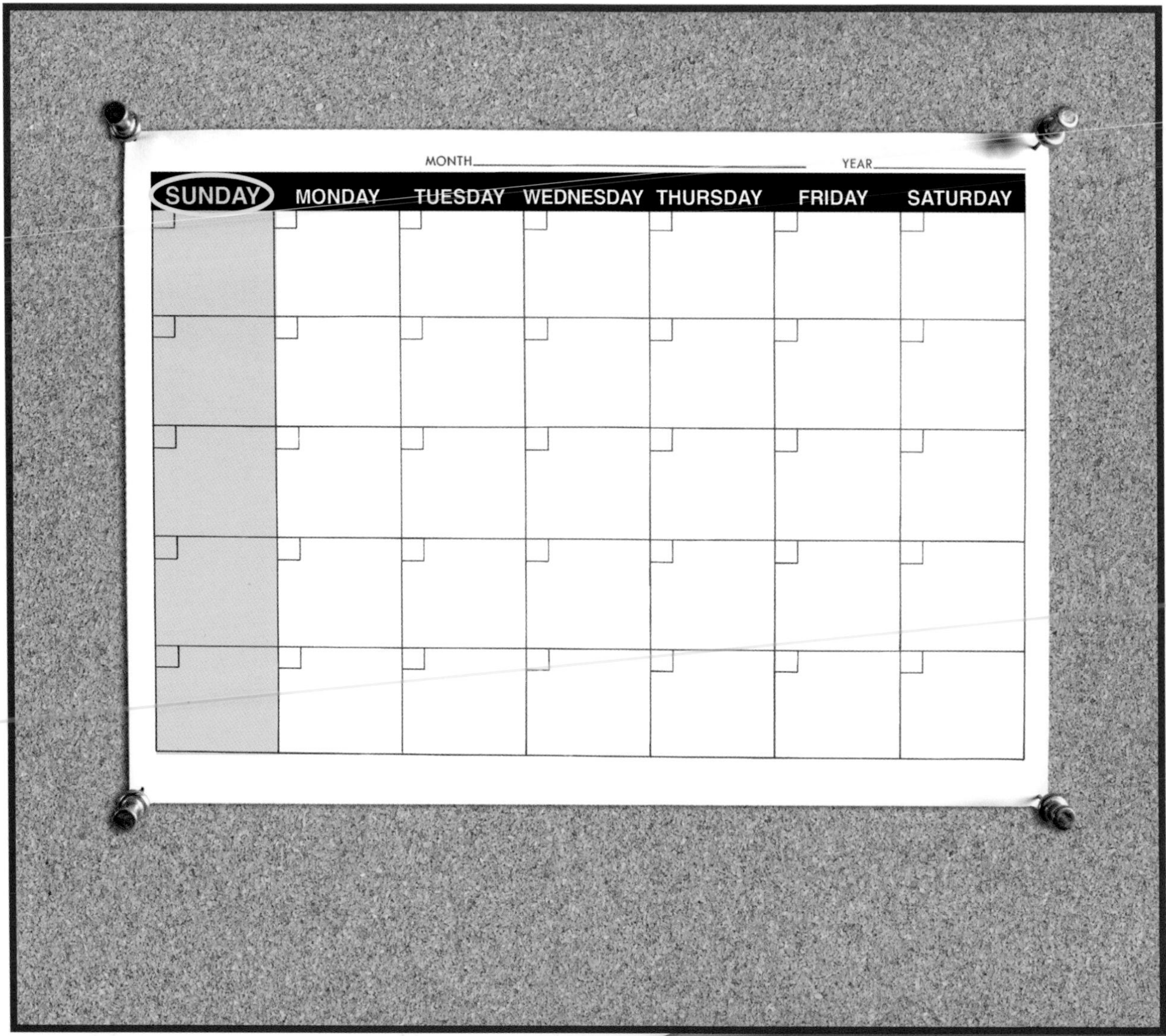

Monday, Tuesday, Wednesday, Thursday, and Friday are weekdays.

Saturday is the last day of the week. Then it is time to start a new week.

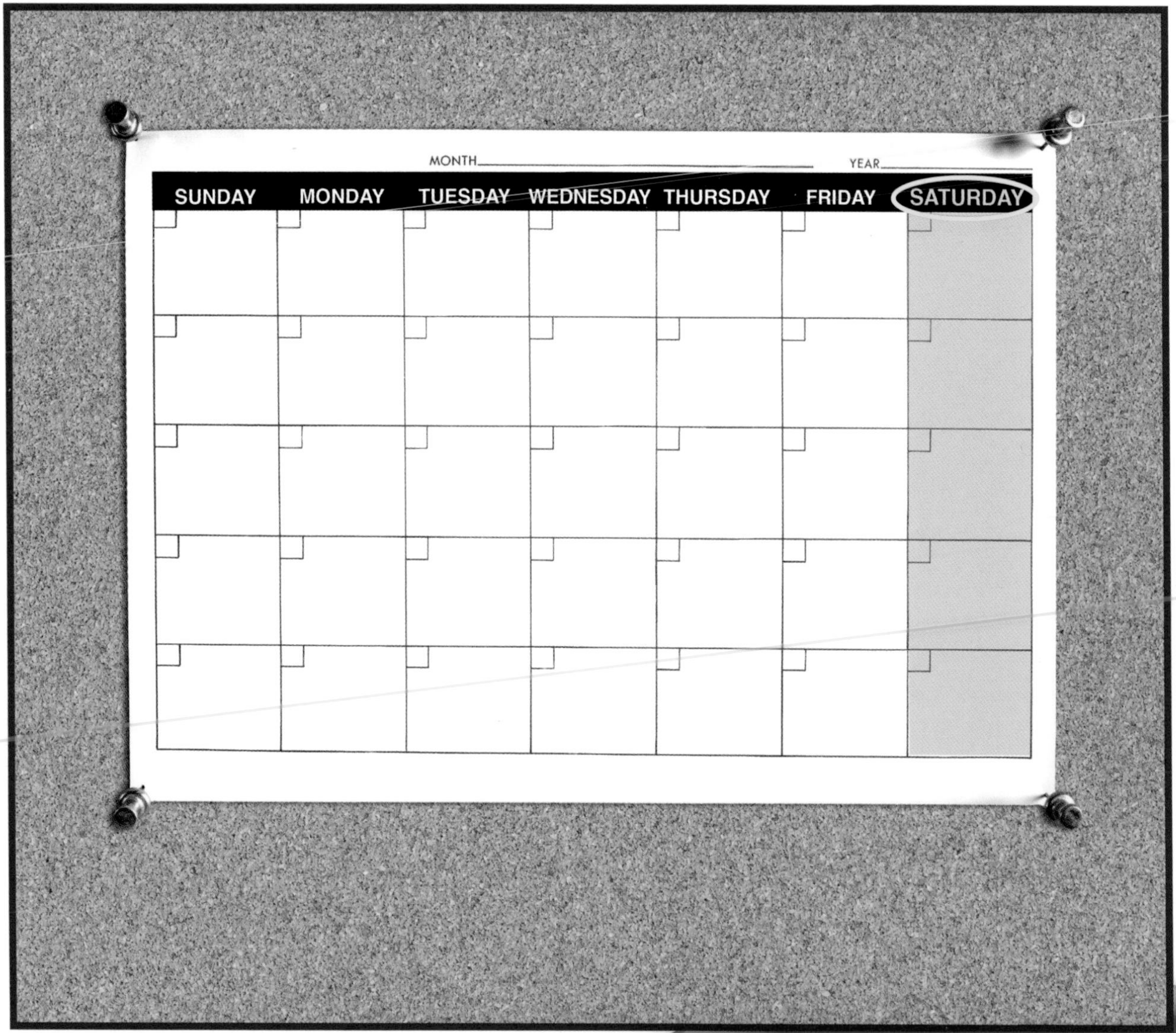

A month can have 28 to 31 days.

January 2014

S	M	T	W	T	F	S
			1	2	3	4
5	6	7	8	9	10	11
12	13	14	15	16	17	18
19	20	21	22	23	24	25
26	27	28	29	30	31	

February 2014

S	M	T	W	T	F	S
						1
2	3	4	5	6	7	8
9	10	11	12	13	14	15
16	17	18	19	20	21	22
23	24	25	26	27	28	

March 2014

S	M	T	W	T	F	S
						1
2	3	4	5	6	7	8
9	10	11	12	13	14	15
16	17	18	19	20	21	22
23	24	25	26	27	28	29
30	31					

April 2014

S	M	T	W	T	F	S
		1	2	3	4	5
6	7	8	9	10	11	12
13	14	15	16	17	18	19
20	21	22	23	24	25	26
27	28	29	30			

May 2014

S	M	T	W	T	F	S
				1	2	3
4	5	6	7	8	9	10
11	12	13	14	15	16	17
18	19	20	21	22	23	24
25	26	27	28	29	30	31

June 2014

S	M	T	W	T	F	S
1	2	3	4	5	6	7
8	9	10	11	12	13	14
15	16	17	18	19	20	21
22	23	24	25	26	27	28
29	30					

July 2014

S	M	T	W	T	F	S
		1	2	3	4	5
6	7	8	9	10	11	12
13	14	15	16	17	18	19
20	21	22	23	24	25	26
27	28	29	30	31		

August 2014

S	M	T	W	T	F	S
					1	2
3	4	5	6	7	8	9
10	11	12	13	14	15	16
17	18	19	20	21	22	23
24	25	26	27	28	29	30
31						

September 2014

S	M	T	W	T	F	S
	1	2	3	4	5	6
7	8	9	10	11	12	13
14	15	16	17	18	19	20
21	22	23	24	25	26	27
28	29	30				

October 2014

S	M	T	W	T	F	S
			1	2	3	4
5	6	7	8	9	10	11
12	13	14	15	16	17	18
19	20	21	22	23	24	25
26	27	28	29	30	31	

November 2014

S	M	T	W	T	F	S
						1
2	3	4	5	6	7	8
9	10	11	12	13	14	15
16	17	18	19	20	21	22
23	24	25	26	27	28	29
30						

December 2014

S	M	T	W	T	F	S
	1	2	3	4	5	6
7	8	9	10	11	12	13
14	15	16	17	18	19	20
21	22	23	24	25	26	27
28	29	30	31			

That's a little more than 4 weeks.

How do we keep track of time? With a calendar!

A calendar is a chart. It shows all the days in a month.

A year has 12 months. The first month is January. The last month is December.

The party is in the month of April on the 11th day.

Hooray! Today is the day we've been waiting for.

The party will be so much fun. Surprise!

And tomorrow is a new day. So you see, time does not stop.

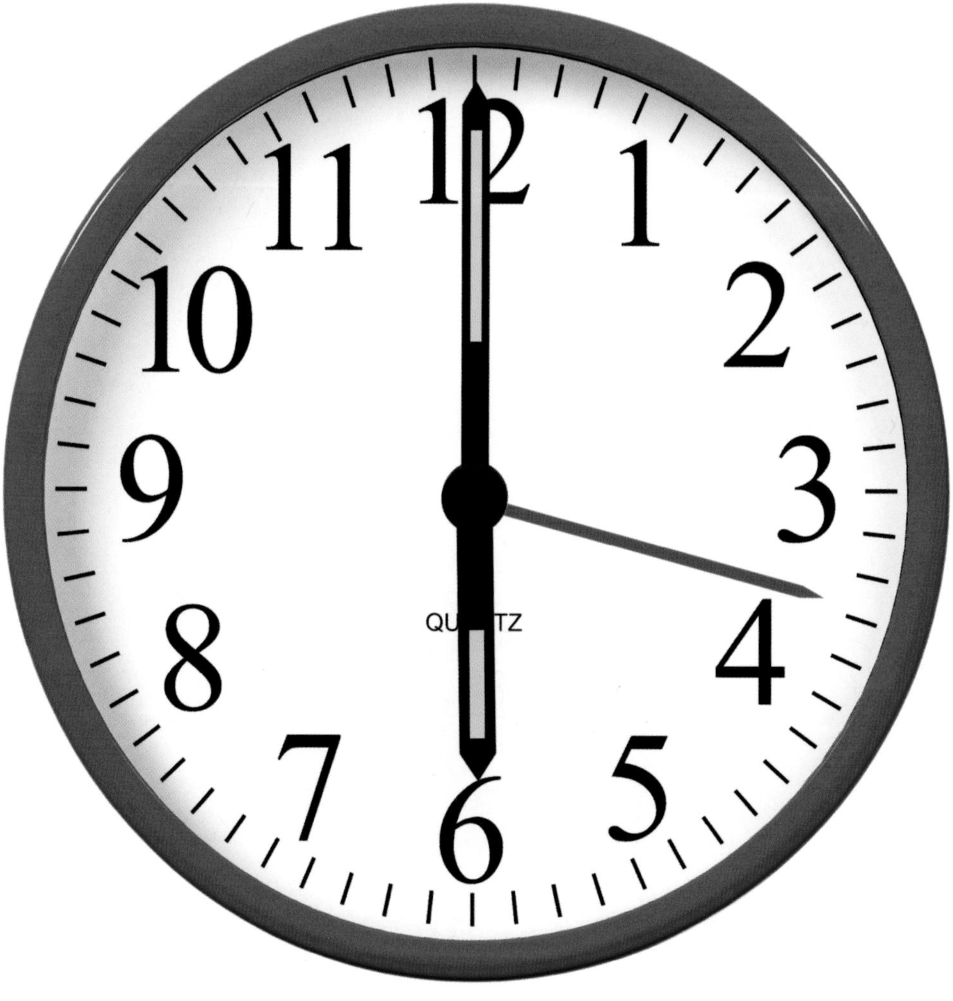

But it is easy to keep track of time by knowing the days, weeks, and months.

Index

Websites

www.abcya.com/days_of_the_week.htm
www.starfall.com/n/holiday/calendar/play.htm?f
www.cookie.com/kids/games/12-months.html

About the Author

Ann H. Matzke works Monday through Friday as a children's librarian. She has an MFA in Writing for Children and Young Adults from Hamline University. In the summer, she enjoys traveling with her family to new places. She likes to read and write books for young readers.

Meet The Author!
www.meetREMauthors.com